Tips & Techniques for Fabulous Fun!

by
Jo Packham & Lisa Groen

Balloon Animals:
Tips & Techniques for Fabulous Fun!
by Jo Packham & Lisa Groen

Balloon Twister: Jenny Nielson--Daisy the Clown
Photography: Ryne Hazen, Hazen Studios
Art Director: Matt Shay, Shay Design

Metric Conversion Chart: Please see page 32

Published by
Mud Puddle, Inc.
36 W. 25th Street
New York, NY 10010
info@mudpuddleinc.com

ISBN: 978-1-60311-360-1

Printed in China, May 2019

13 15 17 19 20 18 16 14

contents

introduction

Welcome to the art of balloon twisting! With a few twists, folds, and turns, a balloon can become any animal you imagine, and a few insects too. The balloon sculptures featured in these pages come with straightforward step-by-step instructions. As you'll notice, they're symmetrical—whatever you do on one side of the balloon, you usually do on the other side. Of course, everyone makes a few unrecognizable figures when they first start. Keep at it. Have fun. In no time, you'll be creating balloon menageries that will entertain partygoers and delight your family *and* friends!

Balloon Basics

MATERIALS

Be sure to use high-quality balloons, which are more durable and less likely to break. Look for balloons manufactured by reputable companies. Long skinny twisting balloons come in different sizes identified by a three-digit number. The first digit represents the diameter of the balloon when inflated, and the last two digits specify the length of the balloon. For example, one of the most popular balloons for twisting is the 260 (2"/5cm diameter, 60"/152cm length).

Bags of balloons may be purchased in one color or multiple colors and typically come in quantities of 100, 144 or 500.

INFLATION

When blowing up long balloons, following a few tips makes the process easier. First, loosen up the balloon by pulling on both ends. Then, squeeze the balloon between your thumb and index finger about an inch or two from the opening. Hold the balloon with your other hand at the opening and blow up just that section. Continue to blow, stretching the balloon away from you as you inflate it.

You will need several breaths to fill the balloon, but be sure to leave an inch or two of room at the end. This allows the air to move while you're twisting it.

When making many balloon animals, use a pump instead. Hold the balloon firmly on the pump as you inflate the balloon.

TYING THE KNOT

After inflating a balloon, let out a small amount or *burp* of air to soften and prevent it from popping. Wrap the open end of the balloon around your index and middle fingers. Using your other hand, pull the opening of the balloon through the circle to tie it off.

Safety

Be sure to take some precautions while making balloon figures:

- When blowing up balloons yourself, place the palm of your hand over the balloon to protect your eyes in case it breaks and snaps back at you.
- To avoid similar accidents when twisting balloons, hold them away from your face.
- Keep your nails short while working with balloons to avoid unnecessary popping. Some people also use a small amount of hand cream to soften their hands before working with balloons.
- No matter what precautions you take, balloons do sometimes pop. If the noise bothers you, earplugs are helpful.
- Pick up any balloons fragments off the floor to keep small children and animals from swallowing them.

twists

Always begin balloon twists at the front of the balloon, which allows the inflated air to move toward the end of the balloon. Also, be sure your twists turn in the same direction—clockwise or counterclockwise—or the sculpture will come loose and you'll have to start over again.

basic twist

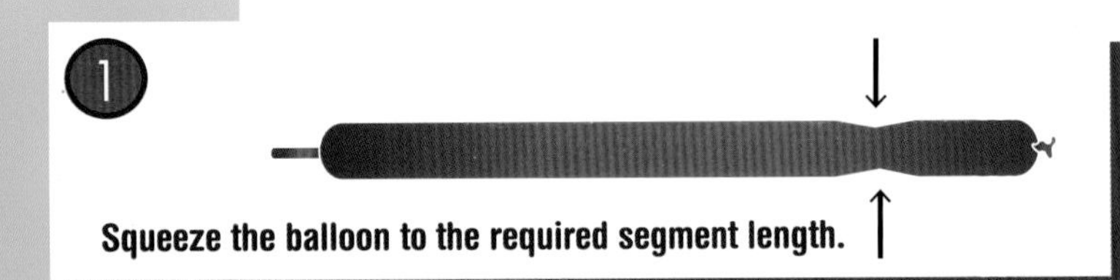

1

Squeeze the balloon to the required segment length.

2

With one hand, hold the end of the balloon, while the other hand twists the balloon three times.

3

When creating several segments in a row, hold onto the first and last segments. You may need someone to help you.

lock twist

A lock twist makes the balloon segments stay in place.
To practice, make a 1" segment followed by two 2" segments.

2

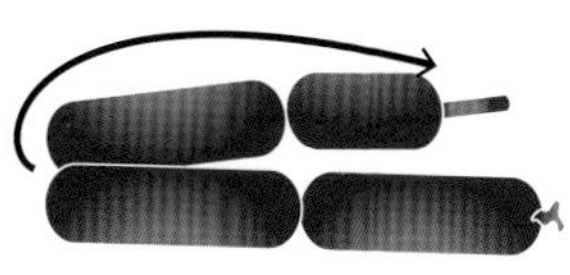

Fold the two 2" segments side by side
at the joint where they are connected.

3

Carefully lift the two segments and twist
three times at their corresponding joints.
This will hold the segments in place.

fold twist

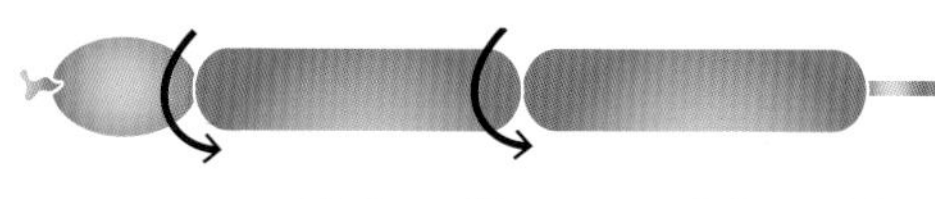

Twist a 1" segment followed by a 3" segment.

2

Lift the large segment and fold it in half.
Twist three times at the two joints.

boomer *the dog*

1

Blow up balloon leaving 2" at the end.

2

HEAD: Twist one 2" section (A) and two 1" sections (B) and (C).

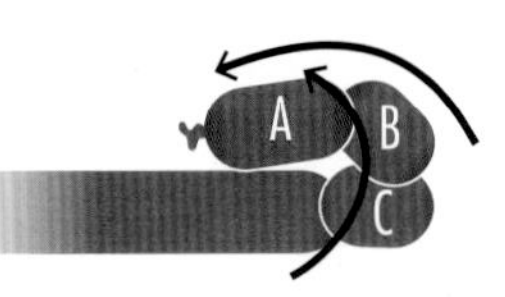

Fold (A) against balloon.
Lock Twist (B) and (C).

HEAD

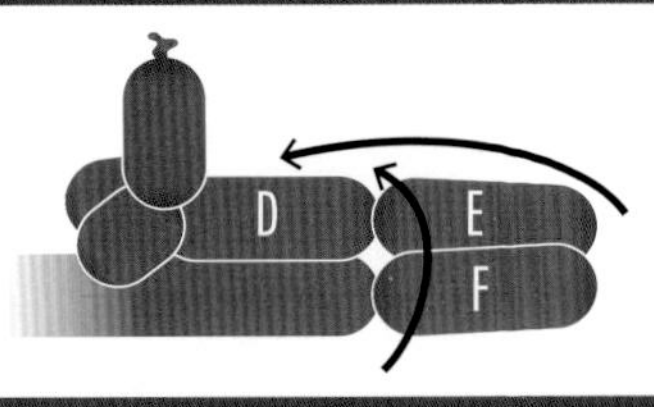

Twist three 3" sections (D, E, F).
Fold (F) against balloon.
Lock Twist (E) and (F).

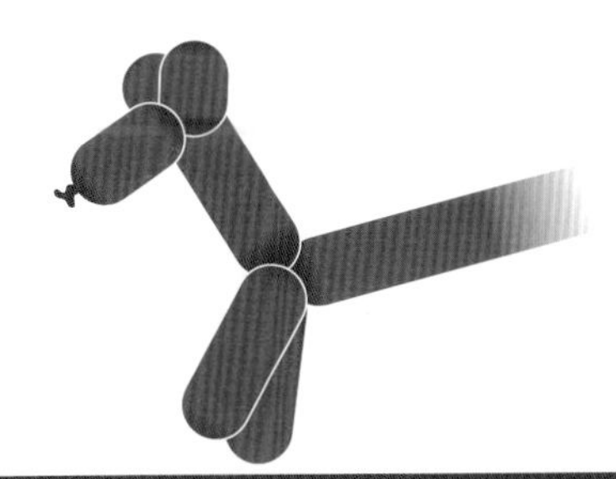

LEGS

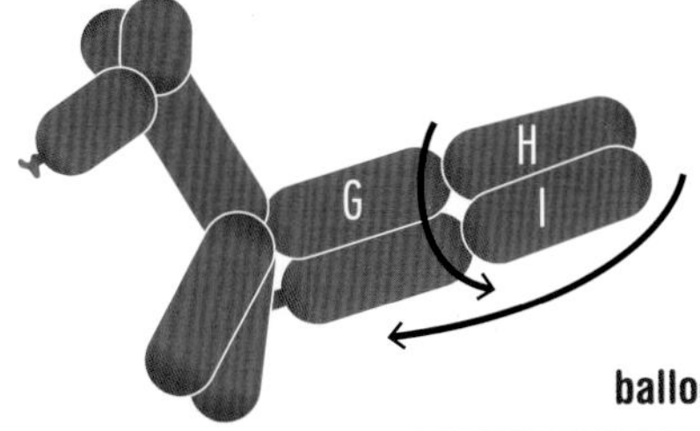

Twist three 3" sections (G, H, I). Fold (I) against balloon. Lock Twist (H) and (I).

slither *the cobra*

Blow up balloon.
Let out air to make it pliable. Holding onto the end, wind the balloon around two fingers without overlapping.

Blow up balloon around fingers to make tight spiral. Tie knot.

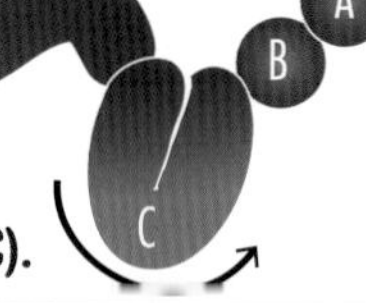

Twist two 2" sections (A) and (B).
Fold twist one 4" section—making 2" head (C).

Push (A) through (C).

balloon bits...

- Hold the balloon at either the front or the already twisted segments, and work toward the end of the balloon.
- Buy top-quality twisting balloons. Less expensive balloons are more fragile and prone to popping.

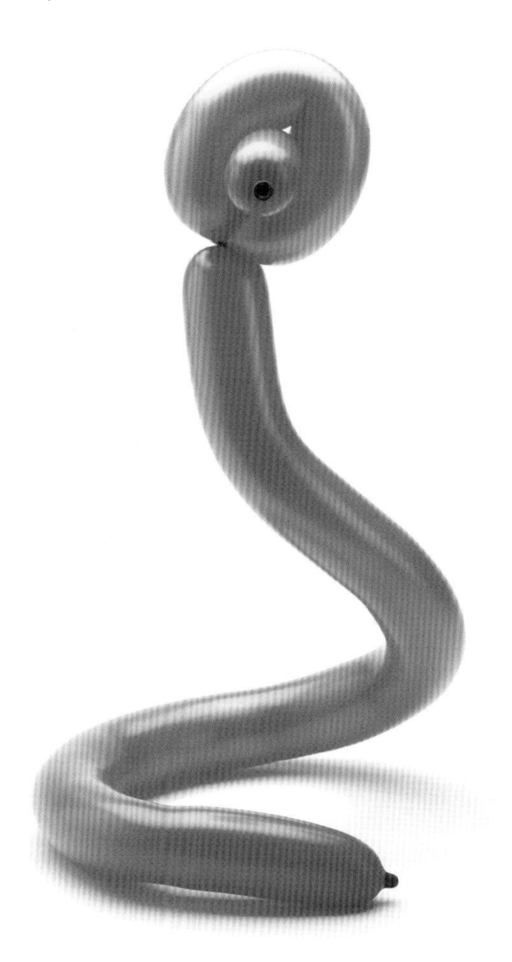

zip the hummingbird

Blow up balloon leaving 2" at the end.

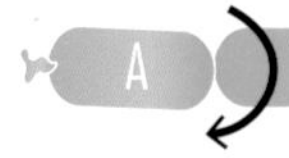

Twist one 2" section (A).

On the other end of balloon, twist one 2" section (B).

4

On tail end, fold twist one 1" section (C).

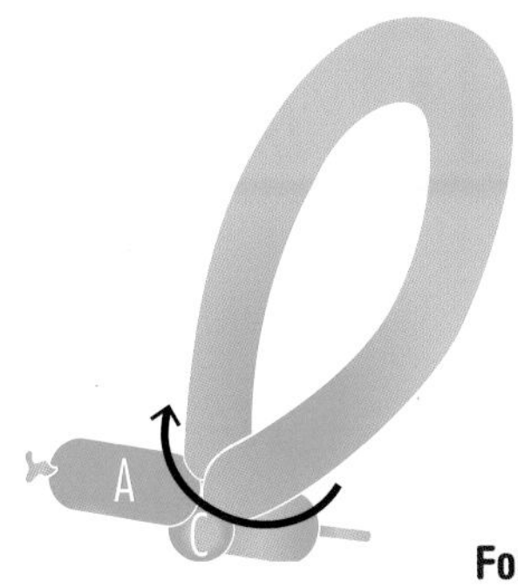

Form loop. Lock twist (C) with (A) .

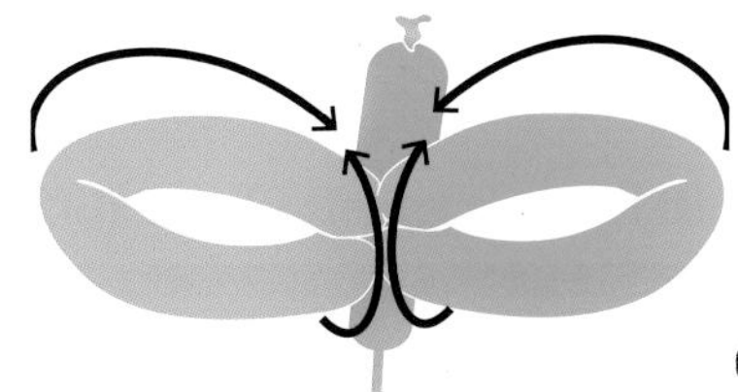

WINGS: Fold twist loop in the center point. Adjust as needed.

stretch *the giraffe*

1

Inflate the balloon leaving 2" at the end.

2

NOSE and EARS:
Twist one 3" segment (A). Twist two 1" segments (B) and (C).

3

Fold (A) against balloon.
Lock twist (B) and (C).

4

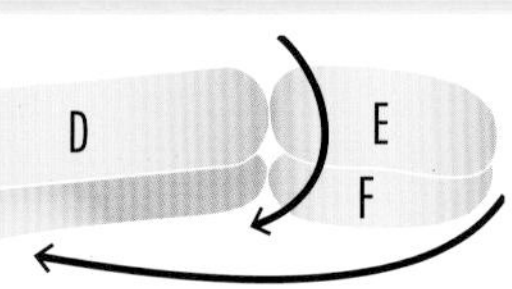

NECK: Twist one 5" section (D). FRONT LEGS: Twist two 3" sections (E) and (F). Fold (F) over (E). Lock twist.

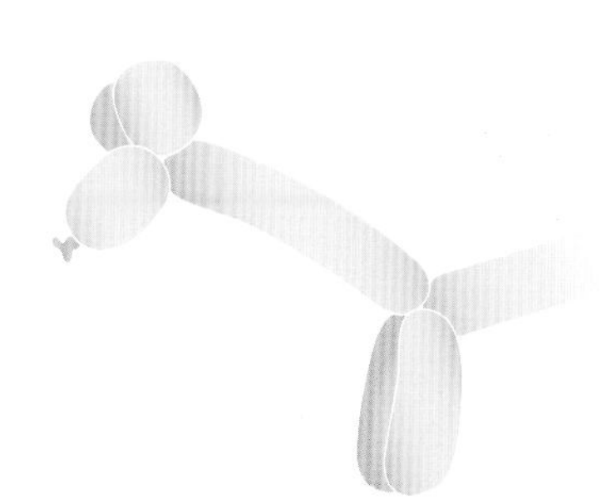

HEAD, NECK, and FRONT LEGS

6

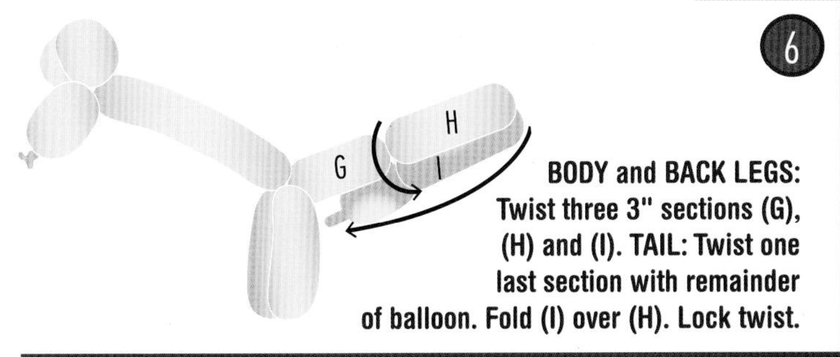

BODY and BACK LEGS:
Twist three 3" sections (G), (H) and (I). TAIL: Twist one last section with remainder of balloon. Fold (I) over (H). Lock twist.

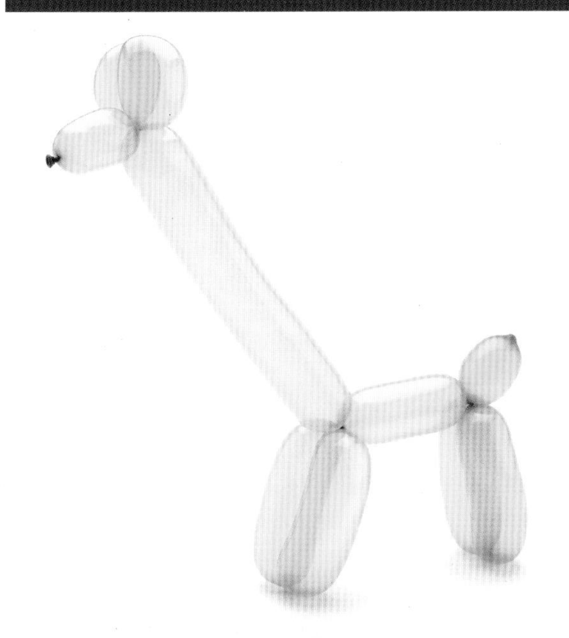

hopper *the rabbit*

1

Blow up balloon leaving 3" at the end.

2

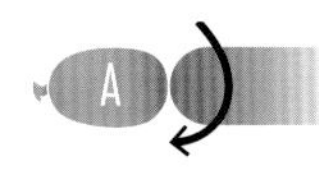

NOSE: Twist one 1" section (A).

3

EARS: Twist two 3" sections (B) and (C).
HEAD: Fold (A) against balloon. Lock twist (B) and (C).

NECK: Twist one 2" section (D).

5

FRONT LEGS: Twist two 3" sections (E) and (F). Fold (F) against (E). Lock twist at neck (D).

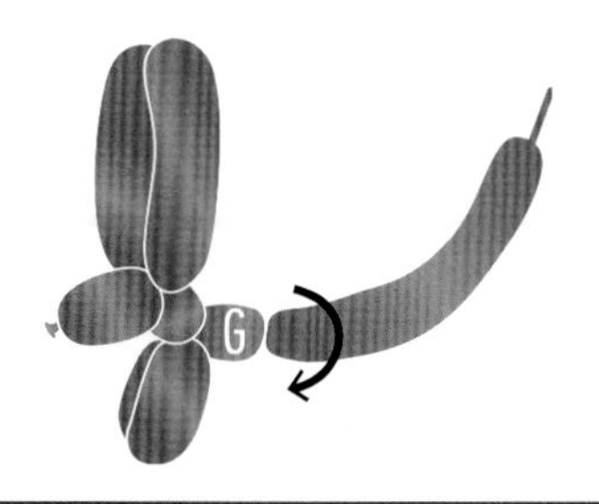

BODY: Twist one 3" section (G).

BACK LEGS and TAIL: Loop all but last 2" of balloon (H). Twist at body (G). Pull front legs into loop. Tail is remainder of balloon.

flutter *the butterfly*

1

Blow up balloon leaving 2" at the end.

2

Twist one 2" section (A) at the front and one 4" section at the end (B).

3

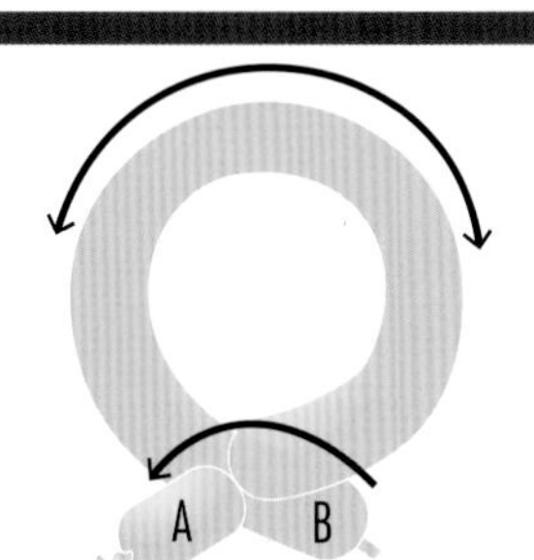

Loop balloon. Lock twist (A) and (B).

4

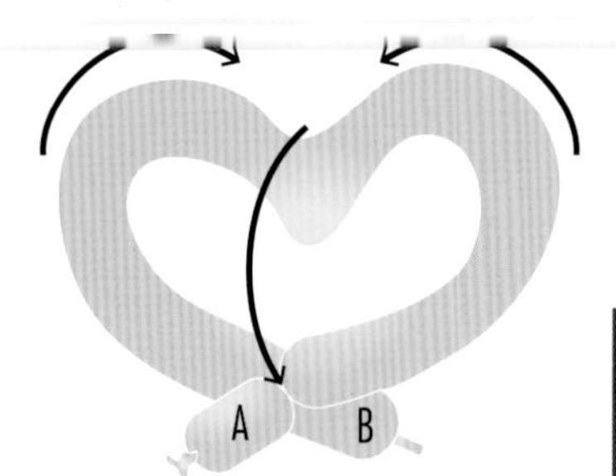

WINGS: Pinch middle of loop. Lock twist to (A) and (B).

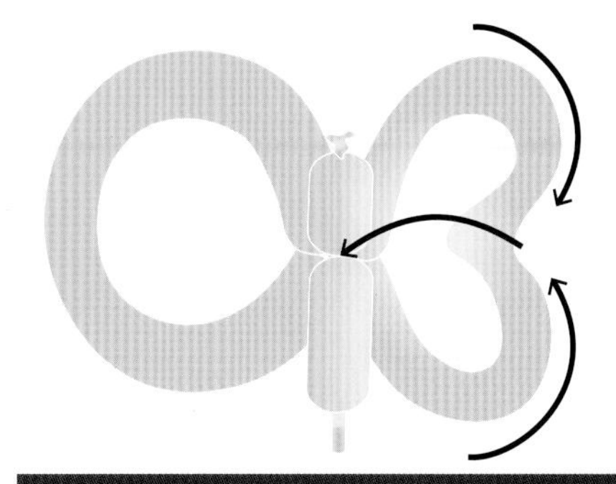

Fold twist middle of left wing to shape.

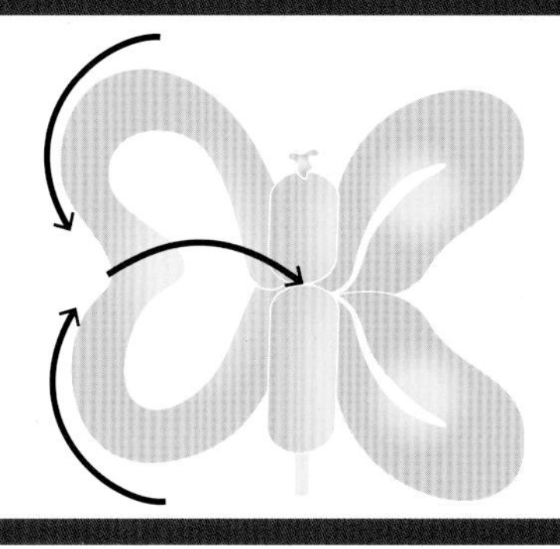

Fold twist middle of right wing to shape.

paulette *the poodle*

Blow up balloon leaving 6" at the end.

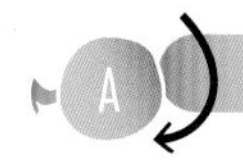

SNOUT: Twist one 1" section (A).

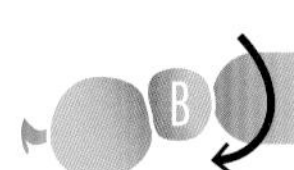

Twist one ½" section (B).

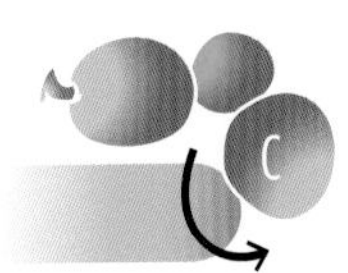

Twist one 1" section (C).

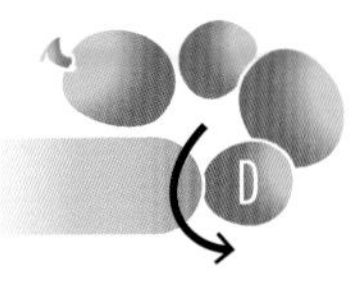

Twist one ½" section (D).

6

HEAD: Lock twist (B) and (D).

7

NECK: Twist one 1" section (E).

8

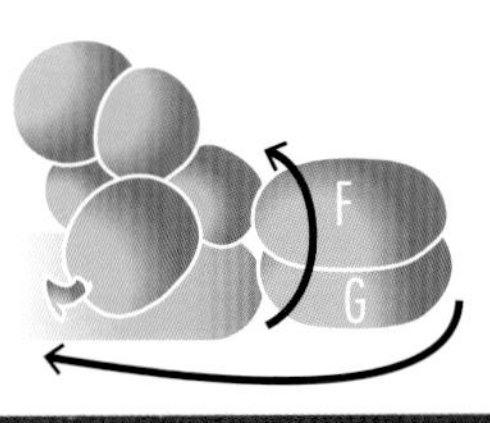

FRONT LEGS: Twist two 2" sections (F) and (G). Lock twist (F) and (G) to body (E).

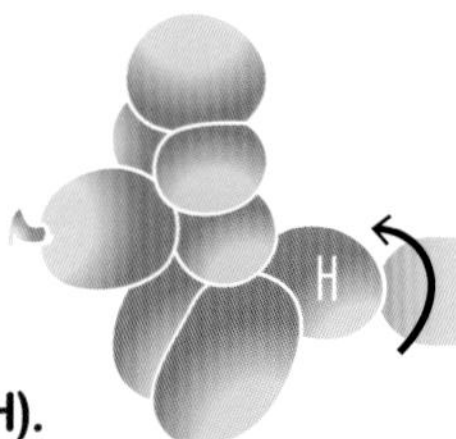

BODY: Twist one 1" section (H).

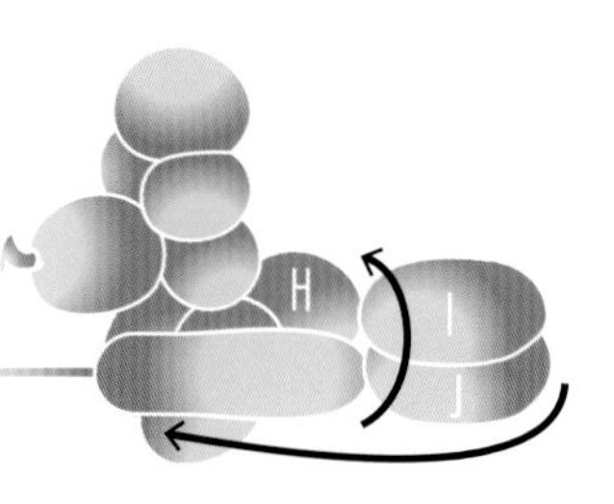

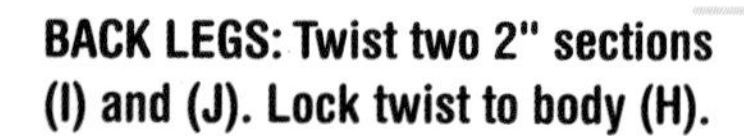

BACK LEGS: Twist two 2" sections (I) and (J). Lock twist to body (H).

**TAIL: Remainder of balloon.
Pull air into uninflated part of tail.**

balloon bits...

- Did you know that the earliest balloon twisters used the intestines of animals? Today balloons are made from special latex that is derived from the sap of a rubber tree in Malaysia.

- Before twisting balloons to entertain people for the first time, rehearse in front of a mirror. Try not to watch your hands so you can make eye contact with your audience.

- Watch balloon twisters on video to learn new techniques. YouTube.com is a great source for brushing up on your skills.

prince *the frog*

1

Blow up balloon leaving 6" at the end.

2

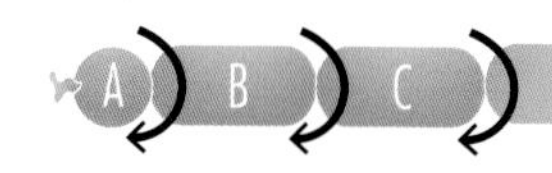

Twist one 1" section (A). Twist two 2" sections (B) and (C).

3

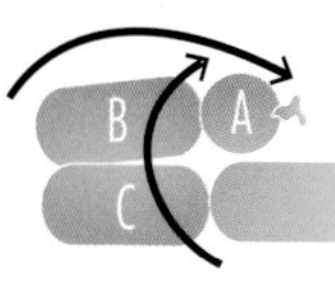

EYES: Fold (C) over (B). Lock twist at (A).

4

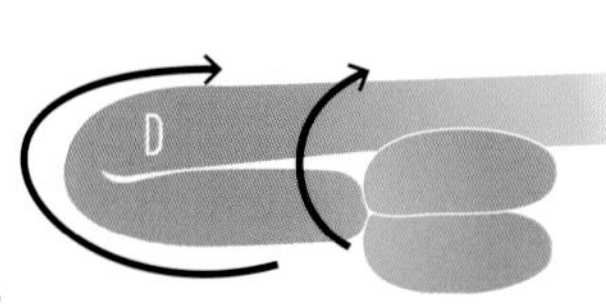

Form 6" loop (D). Lock twist.

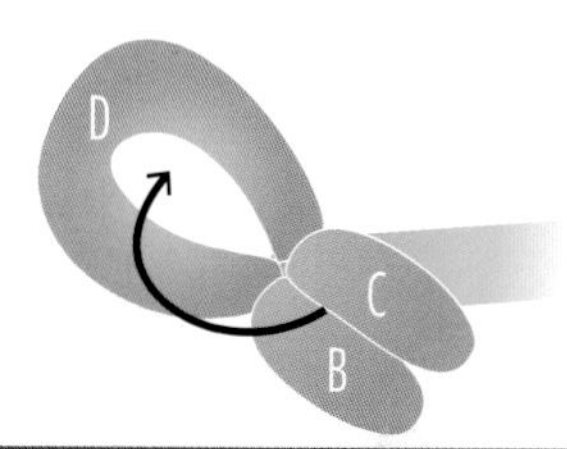

Pull eyes (B) and (C) through loop (D).

FACE

ARMS: Twist two 3" sections (E) and (F). Fold (F) over (E). Lock twist legs to face (D).

balloon bits...

- If your balloons keep popping, are they overinflated? Is there enough room in the tail for twisting?

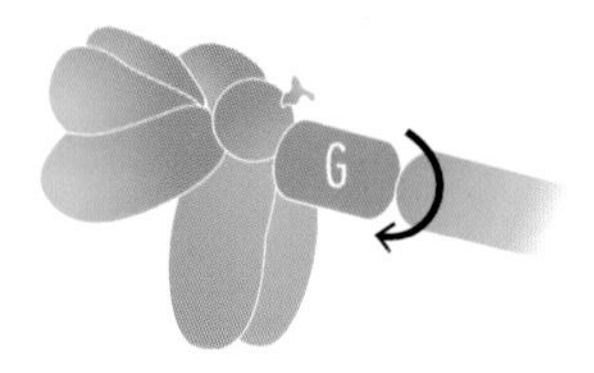

BODY: Twist one 1" section (G).

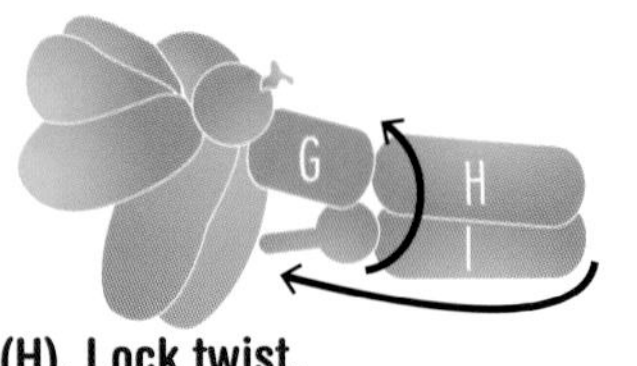

Twist two 3" sections (H) and (I).
TAIL: Twist one last section with remainder of balloon. Fold (I) over (H). Lock twist.

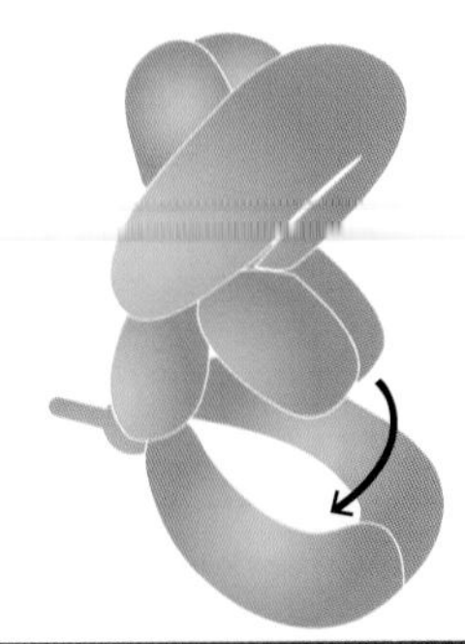

SITTING OPTION:
Place arms (E) and (F) inside loop (H).

balloon bits...

- When attempting a balloon figure for the first time, underinflate your balloon to make it softer and more pliable.
- Experienced balloon entertainers usually designate one hand for holding the balloon and the other for twisting it.
- When using markers to draw whiskers, eyes, or spots on the balloons, avoid ink that that contains alcohol, which disintegrates rubber.
- Store balloons in a cool, dry place to preserve them, away from the light.

leo *the lion*

1

Blow up balloon leaving 2" at the end.

2

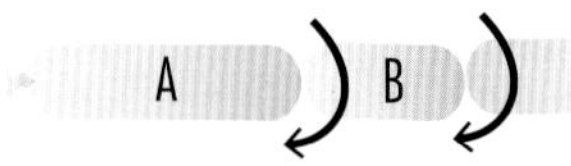

Twist one 4" section (A) and one 2" section (B).

3

Twist one 1" section (C). Fold (C) over (B). Lock twist.

4

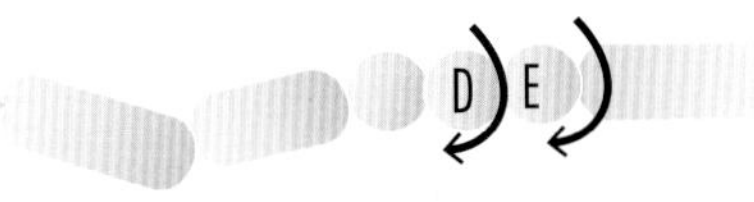

Twist two 1" sections (D) and (E). Fold (E) over (D). Lock twist.

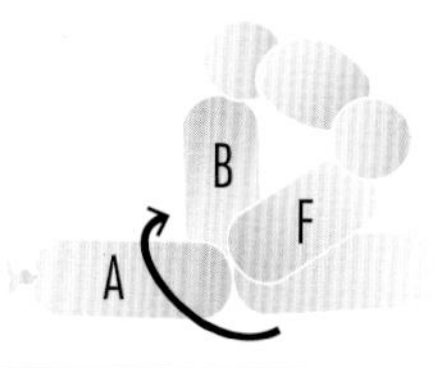

Twist one 2" section (F) and lock twist to (A).

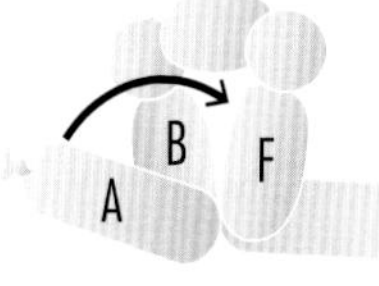

NOSE and CHEEKS: Push (A) through (B) and (F).

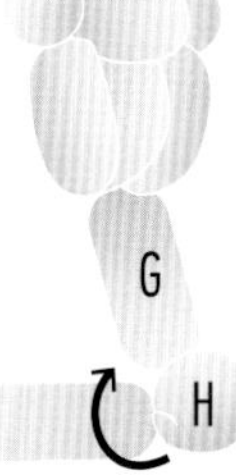

1st LEG and PAW: Twist one 4" section (G), and one 1" section (H). Fold (H) over (G). Lock twist.

8

2ND LEG and PAW: Twist one 1" section (I). Fold over (G). Lock twist. Twist one 4" section (J). Lock twist to cat's head.

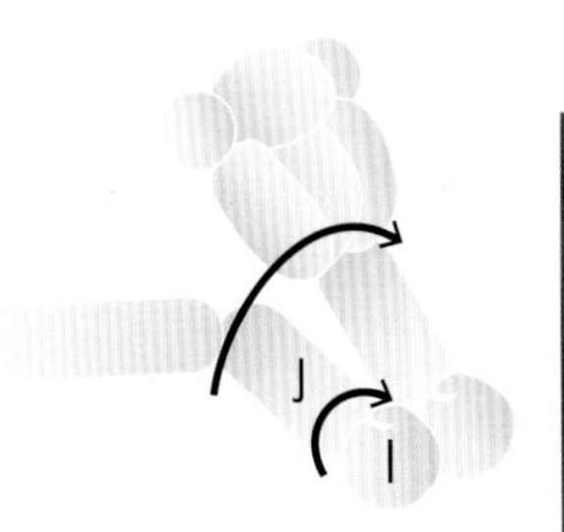

9

BODY and BACK LEGS: Twist one 6" section (K) and two 4" sections (L) and (M). Fold N over M. Lock twist at body (K). TAIL: Remainder of balloon.

10

SITTING CAT: Separate the back legs slightly (L) and (M) and place front legs inside of circle.

balloon bits...

- Soften your fingernails with an emery board to prevent balloon popping.
- If your hands are small, you may find it easier to work with thinner balloons, such as the 160 size.
- When a project has more twists, you will need more air in the tail or the tip of the balloon.

entertaining a party?

After you've mastered a repertoire of balloon creatures, don't be surprised if people ask you to come to their parties. Here are a few tips to help you transition from hobbyist to entertainer:

- When entertaining, wear a colorful costume.
- Bring a balloon pump to inflate your balloons. A party requires many balloons and you'll run out of breath quickly.
- Bring a small table, like a magician's table, to keep supplies and—where appropriate—a container for tips.
- Have business cards on hand, in case someone wants to hire you for a future party.

Metric Conversion Chart

U.S.	Metric
½"	1.3 cm
1"	2.5 cm
2"	5 cm
3"	7.6 cm
4"	10 cm
5"	12.7 cm
6"	15 cm
8"	20 cm